PRONOUNS SAY "YOU AND ME!"

by Michael Dahl

illustrated by Lauren Lowen

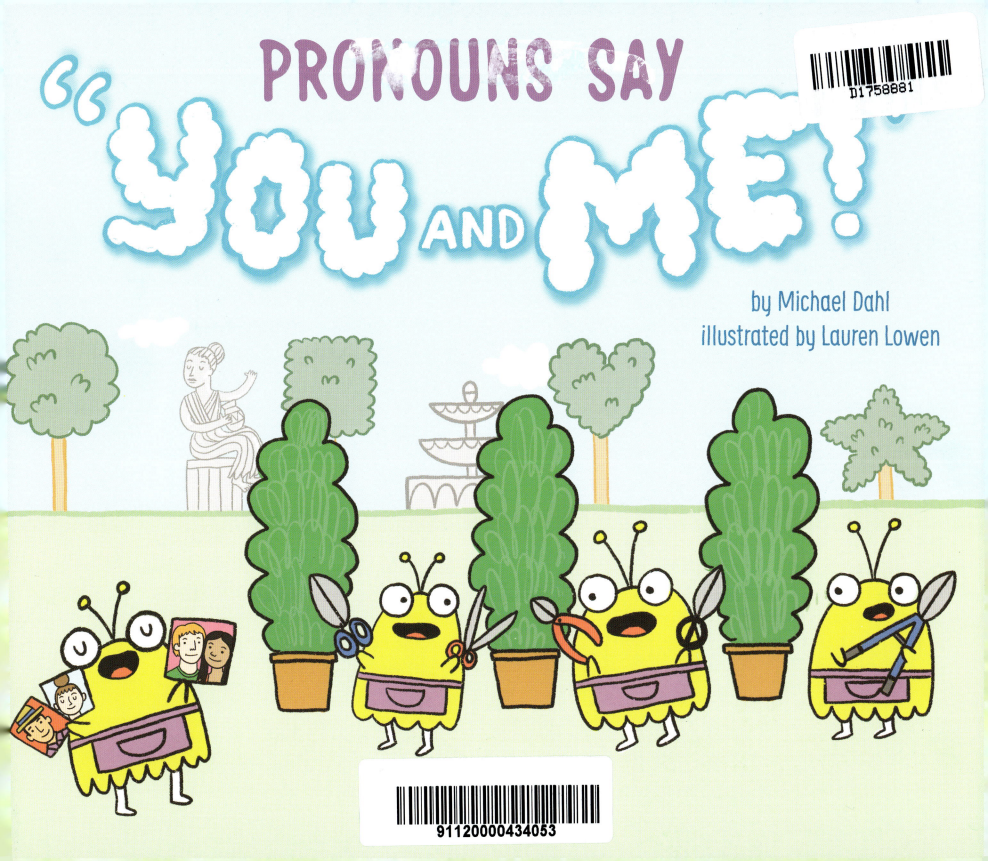

Pronouns are very busy, hardworking words.

3

4

Pronouns are quite attached to nouns. In fact, the word "pronoun" has the word "noun" in it.

A pronoun takes the place of a noun — a person, place or thing. It can also take the place of more than one noun.

12

13

Some pronouns are personal.

"Personal" means "to do with a person or people".

Some pronouns take the place of a person or a person's name.

him   her

he

she

14

15

Personal pronouns can be possessive.

The word "possessive" means "to belong to".

Hmm. Like, why is **MY** worm hanging from **YOUR** mouth?

My pot is so heavy!

Ha! **Your** pot isn't as heavy as **mine** is.

Some pronouns ask questions, such as "who", "whom", "whose", "what" and "which". They're called interrogative pronouns.

"Interrogative" comes from the word "interrogate".

It means "to ask questions".

What is in the dog's mouth?

Whose is **that**?

I am not a liar. I am asking a perfectly simple question!

A lyre.

19

Pronouns come in handy when something is happening to someone.

21

When you don't want to name a specific someone or something, you can use an indefinite pronoun (like "someone" or "something").

Does **anybody** know what's going on?

Somebody must have an idea.

A **few** of the stories sound fishy.

Everybody, settle down!

We saw **something**.

The dog came out of **nowhere**!

23

PRONOUNS

Pronouns take the place of nouns.
Nouns name a person, place or thing.

personal: I, you, she, he, it, we, they, me, her, him, us, them
possessive: mine, yours, hers, his, its, ours, theirs, my, your, her, our, their
interrogative: who, whose, which, what, whom
indefinite: anybody, nowhere, someone, few, none, everything . . . and many more!

And our personal favourite personal pronoun . . .

SOME POINTERS ON PRONOUNS

Pronouns are words that take the place of nouns. A noun *is* a person, place or thing.

> Lulu wore a tutu to school. ("Lulu" and "tutu" are nouns.)
> SHE wore IT to school. ("She" and "it" are pronouns, taking the place of "Lulu" and "tutu.")

Pronouns can take the place of more than one person, place or thing.

> Ivy, Leo, and I tell the funniest jokes.
> WE tell the funniest jokes.
> Captain Cuckoo's Crunch Cookies taste delicious!
> THEY taste delicious!

Personal pronouns take the place of people. Common personal pronouns include "I", "me" and "you".

> YOU want to buy Mimi and Joe a goldfish. I want to buy THEM a parrot. But first, maybe WE should ask THEM if THEY like animals!

Possessive pronouns show ownership.

> The tuba is MINE.
> YOUR bike sparkles!
> The biscuits are THEIRS.
> I wore HIS boots.

Interrogative pronouns ask questions.

> WHOSE dog is more clever?
> WHAT do you want for lunch?
> WHICH should we read?
> WHO has the tickets?

Indefinite pronouns name general people, places and things.

> EVERYBODY knows SOMEONE who has a cat.
> The campsite is in the middle of NOWHERE.
> ANYTHING and EVERYTHING is great!

ABOUT THE AUTHOR

Michael Dahl is the author of more than 200 books for children and has won the AEP Distinguished Achievement Award three times for his non-fiction. He is the author of the bestselling *Bedtime for Batman* and *You're a Star, Wonder Woman!* picture books. He has written dozens of books of jokes, riddles and puns. He likes to play with words. At primary school, he read the dictionary for fun. Really. Michael is proud to say that he has always been a noun. A PROPER noun, at that.

ABOUT THE ILLUSTRATOR

Since graduating from the Illustration Department at the Rhode Island School of Design (RISD), USA, **Lauren Lowen** has been creating art for a variety of projects, including publishing, adverts and products ranging from greeting cards and stickers to activity books and kids' luggage. She taught illustration at both Montserrat College of Art and RISD before becoming an instructor at Watkins College of Art in Nashville, Tennessee, USA, where she currently lives with her husband and son. Some of her favourite things include sushi, chocolate milk and Star Trek.

GLOSSARY

indefinite pronoun a type of pronoun that tells about people and things without being specific

interrogative pronoun a type of pronoun that asks a question

noun a word that names a person, place, or thing

personal to do with a person or people

possessive pronoun a type of pronoun that shows an object belongs to someone or something

pronoun a word that takes the place of a noun

specific clearly defined

THINK ABOUT IT

1. How are personal pronouns and possessive pronouns related?

2. How would you introduce yourself and your family to a stranger without using pronouns?

3. Turn to pages 18 and 19. Use pronouns to describe what the characters are doing. For example, "HE is passing the crisps to HER. THEY are sitting on THEIR picnic blankets."

FIND OUT MORE

Get Set Go: Know Your Grammar, Fran Bromage (Miles Kelly, 2018)

Junior Illustrated Grammar and Punctuation (Illustrated Dictionary), Jane Bingham (Usborne, 2016)

Visual Guide to Grammar and Punctuation (First Reference for Young Writers and Readers), DK (DK Children, 2017)

WEBSITES

BBC Bitesize: Grammar
www.bbc.co.uk/bitesize/topics/zrqqtfr

Grammaropolis: The Pronouns
grammaropolis.com/pronoun.php

LOOK FOR ALL THE PARTS OF SPEECH TITLES

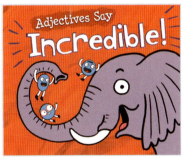

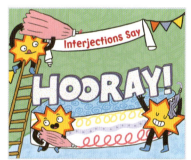
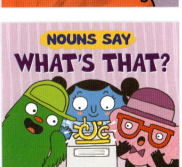

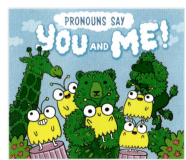

INDEX

Raintree is an imprint of Capstone Global Library Limited, a company incorporated in England and Wales having its registered office at 264 Banbury Road, Oxford, OX2 7DY — Registered company number: 6695582

www.raintree.co.uk
myorders@raintree.co.uk

Text © Capstone Global Library Limited 2020
The moral rights of the proprietor have been asserted.

Edited by Jill Kalz
Designed by Lori Bye
Production by Katy LaVigne
Originated by Capstone Global Library Limited
Printed and bound in India

ISBN 978 1 4747 7485 7

British Library Cataloguing in Publication Data
A full catalogue record for this book is available from the British Library